I0621991

# Meditating on the Luminous Mysteries

## An Intentional Rosary

Amy Schisler

Bozman, MD 2023

# $\mathcal{T}$able of Contents

# *H*ow to use this book

An intentional Rosary is said with a pause before each Hail Mary within the five decades of the Rosary. This pause enables you to insert your own petition or to pray for the needs or prayer requests of others. The petitions in this book are inserted so you may meditate more deeply on the Joyful Mysteries. You may follow the prayers included, or you may substitute your own prayers. A favorite prayer of mine is The Memorare. I always close my Rosary with this prayer. I have included it at the end of the Rosary for your use.

May our Blessed Mother and her Son bestow upon you many blessings as you follow her request to pray the Rosary.

From the United States Conference of Catholic Bishops:
*The Rosary is a Scripture-based prayer. It begins with the Apostles' Creed, which summarizes the great mysteries of the Catholic faith. The Our*

*Father, which introduces each mystery, is from the Gospels. The first part of the Hail Mary is the angel's words announcing Christ's birth and Elizabeth's greeting to Mary. St. Pius V officially added the second part of the Hail Mary. The Mysteries of the Rosary center on the events of Christ's life. There are four sets of Mysteries: Joyful, Sorrowful, Glorious and—added by Saint John Paul II in 2002—the Luminous.*

Typical Days to Pray Each Rosary:
Sunday and Wednesday – Glorious
Monday and Saturday – Joyful
Tuesday and Friday – Sorrowful
Thursday – Luminous

# *T*he Beginning of the Rosary

In the Name of the Father, and of the
Son, and of the Holy Spirit.
Amen

I believe in God,
the Father almighty,
Creator of heaven and earth,
and in Jesus Christ, his only Son, our Lord,
who was conceived by the Holy Spirit,
born of the Virgin Mary,
suffered under Pontius Pilate,
was crucified, died and was buried;
he descended into hell;
on the third day he rose again from the
dead;
he ascended into heaven,
and is seated at the right hand of God the
Father almighty;
from there he will come to judge the living
and the dead.
I believe in the Holy Spirit,
the holy catholic Church,
the communion of saints,
the forgiveness of sins,
the resurrection of the body,

and life everlasting.
Amen.


Our Father, who art in Heaven, hallowed
be thy name.
Thy kingdom come.
Thy will be done on Earth as it is in
Heaven.
Give us this day our daily bread,
And forgive us our trespasses as we
forgive those who trespass against us.
And lead us not into temptation, but
deliver us from evil.
Amen


For the grace of Faith:
Hail Mary, full of grace.
The Lord is with thee.
Blessed art thou among women,
And blessed is the fruit of thy womb,
Jesus.
Holy Mary, Mother of God,
Pray for us sinners,
Now and at the hour of death.
Amen

For the grace of Hope:
Hail Mary, full of grace.
The Lord is with thee.
Blessed art thou among women,
And blessed is the fruit of thy womb,
Jesus.
Holy Mary, Mother of God,
Pray for us sinners,
Now and at the hour of death.
Amen
For the grace of Charity:
Hail Mary, full of grace.
The Lord is with thee.
Blessed art thou among women,
And blessed is the fruit of thy womb,
Jesus.
Holy Mary, Mother of God,
Pray for us sinners,
Now and at the hour of death.
Amen

Glory be to the Father,
And the Son,
And the Holy Spirit,
As now and ever shall be,
World without end.
Amen

# *T*he First Joyful Mystery:
## The Annunciation
Luke 1:26-38

*In the sixth month, the angel Gabriel was sent from God to a town of Galilee called Nazareth, to a virgin betrothed to a man named Joseph, of the house of David, and the virgin's name was Mary.*

*And coming to her, he said, "Hail, favored one! The Lord is with you." But she was greatly troubled at what was said and pondered what sort of greeting this might be. Then the angel said to her, "Do not be afraid, Mary, for you have found favor with God. Behold, you will conceive in your womb and bear a son, and you shall name him Jesus. He will be great and will be called Son of the Most High, and the Lord God will give him the throne of David his father, and he will rule over the house of Jacob forever, and of his kingdom there will be no end."*

*But Mary said to the angel, "How can this be, since I have no relations with a man?"*

*And the angel said to her in reply, "The holy Spirit will come upon you, and the power of the Most High will overshadow you. Therefore the child to be born will be called holy, the Son of God. And behold, Elizabeth, your relative, has also conceived a son in her old age, and this is the sixth month for her who was called barren; or nothing will be impossible for God."*

*Mary said, "Behold, I am the handmaid of the Lord. May it be done to me according to your word." Then the angel departed from her.*

Our Father, who art in Heaven, hallowed be thy name.
Thy kingdom come.
Thy will be done on Earth as it is in Heaven.
Give us this day our daily bread,
And forgive us our trespasses as we forgive those who trespass against us.
And lead us not into temptation, but deliver us from evil.
Amen

*For the health and safety of pregnant mothers and their unborn children:*

Hail Mary, full of grace.
The Lord is with thee.
Blessed art thou among women,
And blessed is the fruit of thy womb,
Jesus.
Holy Mary, Mother of God,
Pray for us sinners,
Now and at the hour of death.
Amen


*For mothers with unplanned pregnancies:*
Hail Mary, full of grace.
The Lord is with thee.
Blessed art thou among women,
And blessed is the fruit of thy womb,
Jesus.
Holy Mary, Mother of God,
Pray for us sinners,
Now and at the hour of death.
Amen


*For mothers without support:*
Hail Mary, full of grace.
The Lord is with thee.
Blessed art thou among women,
And blessed is the fruit of thy womb,

Jesus.
Holy Mary, Mother of God,
Pray for us sinners,
Now and at the hour of death.
Amen

*For pregnant mothers in harmful or desperate situations:*
Hail Mary, full of grace.
The Lord is with thee.
Blessed art thou among women,
And blessed is the fruit of thy womb,
Jesus.
Holy Mary, Mother of God,
Pray for us sinners,
Now and at the hour of death.
Amen

*For mothers experiencing medically difficult pregnancies:*
Hail Mary, full of grace.
The Lord is with thee.
Blessed art thou among women,
And blessed is the fruit of thy womb,
Jesus.
Holy Mary, Mother of God,
Pray for us sinners,

Now and at the hour of death.
Amen

*For babies experiencing medical complications in the womb:*
Hail Mary, full of grace.
The Lord is with thee.
Blessed art thou among women,
And blessed is the fruit of thy womb,
Jesus.
Holy Mary, Mother of God,
Pray for us sinners,
Now and at the hour of death.
Amen

*For pregnant mothers unsure of their future:*
Hail Mary, full of grace.
The Lord is with thee.
Blessed art thou among women,
And blessed is the fruit of thy womb,
Jesus.
Holy Mary, Mother of God,
Pray for us sinners,
Now and at the hour of death.
Amen

*For loving support of all spouses during and after pregnancy:*
Hail Mary, full of grace.
The Lord is with thee.
Blessed art thou among women,
And blessed is the fruit of thy womb,
Jesus.
Holy Mary, Mother of God,
Pray for us sinners,
Now and at the hour of death.
Amen

*For mothers carrying unwanted babies, especially those considering termination:*
Hail Mary, full of grace.
The Lord is with thee.
Blessed art thou among women,
And blessed is the fruit of thy womb,
Jesus.
Holy Mary, Mother of God,
Pray for us sinners,
Now and at the hour of death.
Amen

*For mothers without any support during or after their pregnancy:*
Hail Mary, full of grace.

The Lord is with thee.
Blessed art thou among women,
And blessed is the fruit of thy womb,
Jesus.
Holy Mary, Mother of God,
Pray for us sinners,
Now and at the hour of death.
Amen

Glory be to the Father,
And the Son,
And the Holy Spirit,
As now and ever shall be,
World without end.
Amen

O my Jesus, forgive us our sins, save us from the fires of hell; lead all souls to Heaven, especially those who have most need of your mercy.

# *T*he Second Joyful Mystery:
## The Visitation
Luke 1:39-45

*During those days Mary set out and traveled to the hill country in haste to a town of Judah, where she entered the house of Zechariah and greeted Elizabeth.*

*When Elizabeth heard Mary's greeting, the infant leaped in her womb, and Elizabeth, filled with the holy Spirit, cried out in a loud voice and said, "Most blessed are you among women, and blessed is the fruit of your womb. And how does this happen to me, that the mother of my Lord should come to me? For at the moment the sound of your greeting reached my ears, the infant in my womb leaped for joy. Blessed are you who believed that what was spoken to you by the Lord would be fulfilled."*

Our Father, who art in Heaven, hallowed be thy name.
Thy kingdom come.
Thy will be done on Earth as it is in Heaven.

Give us this day our daily bread,
And forgive us our trespasses as we
forgive those who trespass against us.
And lead us not into temptation, but
deliver us from evil.
Amen

*For the safety of mothers who must immigrate or
travel during pregnancy:*
Hail Mary, full of grace.
The Lord is with thee.
Blessed art thou among women,
And blessed is the fruit of thy womb,
Jesus.
Holy Mary, Mother of God,
Pray for us sinners,
Now and at the hour of death.
Amen


*For pregnant mothers who feel afraid for any
reason:*
Hail Mary, full of grace.
The Lord is with thee.
Blessed art thou among women,
And blessed is the fruit of thy womb,
Jesus.
Holy Mary, Mother of God,

Pray for us sinners,
Now and at the hour of death.
Amen

*For those who care for pregnant mothers:*
Hail Mary, full of grace.
The Lord is with thee.
Blessed art thou among women,
And blessed is the fruit of thy womb,
Jesus.
Holy Mary, Mother of God,
Pray for us sinners,
Now and at the hour of death.
Amen

*For pregnant mothers without help or guidance:*
Hail Mary, full of grace.
The Lord is with thee.
Blessed art thou among women,
And blessed is the fruit of thy womb,
Jesus.
Holy Mary, Mother of God,
Pray for us sinners,
Now and at the hour of death.
Amen

*For older, pregnant mothers:*

Hail Mary, full of grace.
The Lord is with thee.
Blessed art thou among women,
And blessed is the fruit of thy womb,
Jesus.
Holy Mary, Mother of God,
Pray for us sinners,
Now and at the hour of death.
Amen

*For women who continue to pray for the gift of children:*
Hail Mary, full of grace.
The Lord is with thee.
Blessed art thou among women,
And blessed is the fruit of thy womb,
Jesus.
Holy Mary, Mother of God,
Pray for us sinners,
Now and at the hour of death.
Amen

*For women who are unable to conceive or carry children:*
Hail Mary, full of grace.
The Lord is with thee.

Blessed art thou among women,
And blessed is the fruit of thy womb,
Jesus.
Holy Mary, Mother of God,
Pray for us sinners,
Now and at the hour of death.
Amen

*For women who have miscarried:*
Hail Mary, full of grace.
The Lord is with thee.
Blessed art thou among women,
And blessed is the fruit of thy womb,
Jesus.
Holy Mary, Mother of God,
Pray for us sinners,
Now and at the hour of death.
Amen

*For all those who work and volunteer for pregnancy centers:*
Hail Mary, full of grace.
The Lord is with thee.
Blessed art thou among women,
And blessed is the fruit of thy womb,
Jesus.
Holy Mary, Mother of God,

Pray for us sinners,
Now and at the hour of death.
Amen

*For fathers of unborn children:*
Hail Mary, full of grace.
The Lord is with thee.
Blessed art thou among women,
And blessed is the fruit of thy womb,
Jesus.
Holy Mary, Mother of God,
Pray for us sinners,
Now and at the hour of death.
Amen

Glory be to the Father,
And the Son,
And the Holy Spirit,
As now and ever shall be,
World without end.
Amen

O my Jesus, forgive us our sins, save us
from the fires of hell; lead all souls to
Heaven, especially those who have most
need of your mercy.

# *T*he Third Joyful Mystery:
## The Nativity
Luke 2:4-14

*And Joseph too went up from Galilee from the town of Nazareth to Judea, to the city of David that is called Bethlehem, because he was of the house and family of David, to be enrolled with Mary, his betrothed, who was with child. While they were there, the time came for her to have her child, and she gave birth to her firstborn son. She wrapped him in swaddling clothes and laid him in a manger, because there was no room for them in the inn.*

*Now there were shepherds in that region living in the fields and keeping the night watch over their flock. The angel of the Lord appeared to them and the glory of the Lord shone around them, and they were struck with great fear. The angel said to them, "Do not be afraid; for behold, I proclaim to you good news of great joy that will be for all the people. For today in the city of David a savior has been born for you who is Messiah and Lord. And this will be a sign for you: you will find an infant wrapped in swaddling clothes and lying in a manger."*

*And suddenly there was a multitude of the heavenly host with the angel, praising God and saying: "Glory to God in the highest and on earth peace to those on whom his favor rests."*

Our Father, who art in Heaven, hallowed be thy name.
Thy kingdom come.
Thy will be done on Earth as it is in Heaven.
Give us this day our daily bread,
And forgive us our trespasses as we forgive those who trespass against us.
And lead us not into temptation, but deliver us from evil.
Amen

*For mothers without medical care:*
Hail Mary, full of grace.
The Lord is with thee.
Blessed art thou among women,
And blessed is the fruit of thy womb, Jesus.
Holy Mary, Mother of God,

Pray for us sinners,
Now and at the hour of death.
Amen


*For mothers without a home or place to live:*
Hail Mary, full of grace.
The Lord is with thee.
Blessed art thou among women,
And blessed is the fruit of thy womb,
Jesus.
Holy Mary, Mother of God,
Pray for us sinners,
Now and at the hour of death.
Amen
*For pregnant mothers without husbands to love
and support them:*
Hail Mary, full of grace.
The Lord is with thee.
Blessed art thou among women,
And blessed is the fruit of thy womb,
Jesus.
Holy Mary, Mother of God,
Pray for us sinners,
Now and at the hour of death.
Amen


*For women who will go into labor under stressful*

*conditions:*
Hail Mary, full of grace.
The Lord is with thee.
Blessed art thou among women,
And blessed is the fruit of thy womb,
Jesus.
Holy Mary, Mother of God,
Pray for us sinners,
Now and at the hour of death.
Amen

*For women with other children or family members to care for:*
Hail Mary, full of grace.
The Lord is with thee.
Blessed art thou among women,
And blessed is the fruit of thy womb,
Jesus.
Holy Mary, Mother of God,
Pray for us sinners,
Now and at the hour of death.
Amen

*For babies born with medical complications:*
Hail Mary, full of grace.
The Lord is with thee.

Blessed art thou among women,
And blessed is the fruit of thy womb,
Jesus.
Holy Mary, Mother of God,
Pray for us sinners,
Now and at the hour of death.
Amen

*For babies born without medical care:*
Hail Mary, full of grace.
The Lord is with thee.
Blessed art thou among women,
And blessed is the fruit of thy womb,
Jesus.
Holy Mary, Mother of God,
Pray for us sinners,
Now and at the hour of death.
Amen

*For women who experience extreme pain before or during labor:*
Hail Mary, full of grace.
The Lord is with thee.
Blessed art thou among women,
And blessed is the fruit of thy womb,
Jesus.
Holy Mary, Mother of God,

Pray for us sinners,
Now and at the hour of death.
Amen


*For mothers in labor at this moment:*
Hail Mary, full of grace.
The Lord is with thee.
Blessed art thou among women,
And blessed is the fruit of thy womb,
Jesus.
Holy Mary, Mother of God,
Pray for us sinners,
Now and at the hour of death.
Amen


*For mothers undergoing complicated labor:*
Hail Mary, full of grace.
The Lord is with thee.
Blessed art thou among women,
And blessed is the fruit of thy womb,
Jesus.
Holy Mary, Mother of God,
Pray for us sinners,
Now and at the hour of death.
Amen

Glory be to the Father,
And the Son,
And the Holy Spirit,
As now and ever shall be,
World without end.
Amen

O my Jesus, forgive us our sins, save us from the fires of hell; lead all souls to Heaven, especially those who have most need of your mercy.

# *T*he Fourth Joyful Mystery:
## The Presentation in the Temple
Luke 2:22-38

*When the days were completed for their purification according to the law of Moses, they took him up to Jerusalem to present him to the Lord, just as it is written in the law of the Lord, "Every male that opens the womb shall be consecrated to the Lord," and to offer the sacrifice of "a pair of turtledoves or two young pigeons," in accordance with the dictate in the law of the Lord.*

*Now there was a man in Jerusalem whose name was Simeon. This man was righteous and devout, awaiting the consolation of Israel, and the holy Spirit was upon him. It had been revealed to him by the holy Spirit that he should not see death before he had seen the Messiah of the Lord. He came in the Spirit into the temple; and when the parents brought in the child Jesus to perform the custom of the law in regard to him, he took him into his arms and blessed God, saying:*

*"Now, Master, you may let your servant go in peace, according to your word, for my eyes have seen your salvation, which you prepared in sight of all the peoples, a light for revelation to the Gentiles, and glory for your people Israel."*

*The child's father and mother were amazed at what was said about him; and Simeon blessed them and said to Mary his mother, "Behold, this child is destined for the fall and rise of many in Israel, and to be a sign that will be contradicted (and you yourself a sword will pierce) so that the thoughts of many hearts may be revealed."*

*There was also a prophetess, Anna, the daughter of Phanuel, of the tribe of Asher. She was advanced in years, having lived seven years with her husband after her marriage, and then as a widow until she was eighty-four. She never left the temple, but worshiped night and day with fasting and prayer. And coming forward at that very time, she gave thanks to God and spoke about the child to all who were awaiting the redemption of Jerusalem.*

Our Father, who art in Heaven, hallowed be thy name.

Thy kingdom come.

Thy will be done on Earth as it is in Heaven.

Give us this day our daily bread,

And forgive us our trespasses as we forgive those who trespass against us.

And lead us not into temptation, but deliver us from evil.

Amen

*For parents preparing their children for Baptism:*

Hail Mary, full of grace.

The Lord is with thee.

Blessed art thou among women,

And blessed is the fruit of thy womb, Jesus.

Holy Mary, Mother of God,

Pray for us sinners,

Now and at the hour of death.

Amen

*For babies about to be baptized:*

Hail Mary, full of grace.

The Lord is with thee.

Blessed art thou among women,

And blessed is the fruit of thy womb,
Jesus.
Holy Mary, Mother of God,
Pray for us sinners,
Now and at the hour of death.
Amen

*For those who have never been baptized or
introduced to God's Church:*
Hail Mary, full of grace.
The Lord is with thee.
Blessed art thou among women,
And blessed is the fruit of thy womb,
Jesus.
Holy Mary, Mother of God,
Pray for us sinners,
Now and at the hour of death.
Amen

*For priests and deacons who administer the
sacraments:*
Hail Mary, full of grace.
The Lord is with thee.
Blessed art thou among women,
And blessed is the fruit of thy womb,
Jesus.
Holy Mary, Mother of God,

Pray for us sinners,
Now and at the hour of death.
Amen

*For those who offer what little they have to God:*
Hail Mary, full of grace.
The Lord is with thee.
Blessed art thou among women,
And blessed is the fruit of thy womb,
Jesus.
Holy Mary, Mother of God,
Pray for us sinners,
Now and at the hour of death.
Amen

*For the righteous and devout who continue to await the consolation of Israel:*
Hail Mary, full of grace.
The Lord is with thee.
Blessed art thou among women,
And blessed is the fruit of thy womb,
Jesus.
Holy Mary, Mother of God,
Pray for us sinners,
Now and at the hour of death.
Amen

*For those who are open to the Holy Spirit:*
Hail Mary, full of grace.
The Lord is with thee.
Blessed art thou among women,
And blessed is the fruit of thy womb,
Jesus.
Holy Mary, Mother of God,
Pray for us sinners,
Now and at the hour of death.
Amen

*For those who eagerly await a happy death:*
Hail Mary, full of grace.
The Lord is with thee.
Blessed art thou among women,
And blessed is the fruit of thy womb,
Jesus.
Holy Mary, Mother of God,
Pray for us sinners,
Now and at the hour of death.
Amen

*For all who have gone before us, whose eyes have seen salvation:*
Hail Mary, full of grace.
The Lord is with thee.
Blessed art thou among women,

And blessed is the fruit of thy womb,
Jesus.
Holy Mary, Mother of God,
Pray for us sinners,
Now and at the hour of death.
Amen

*For all who speak to others about Jesus and his gift of redemption:*
Hail Mary, full of grace.
The Lord is with thee.
Blessed art thou among women,
And blessed is the fruit of thy womb,
Jesus.
Holy Mary, Mother of God,
Pray for us sinners,
Now and at the hour of death.
Amen

Glory be to the Father,
And the Son,
And the Holy Spirit,
As now and ever shall be,
World without end.
Amen

O my Jesus, forgive us our sins, save us from the fires of hell; lead all souls to Heaven, especially those who have most need of your mercy.

# *T*he Fifth Joyful Mystery:
## The Finding in the Temple
Luke 2:41-52

*Each year his parents went to Jerusalem for the feast of Passover, and when he was twelve years old, they went up according to festival custom. After they had completed its days, as they were returning, the boy Jesus remained behind in Jerusalem, but his parents did not know it. Thinking that he was in the caravan, they journeyed for a day and looked for him among their relatives and acquaintances, but not finding him, they returned to Jerusalem to look for him.*

*After three days they found him in the temple, sitting in the midst of the teachers, listening to them and asking them questions, and all who heard him were astounded at his understanding and his answers.*

*When his parents saw him, they were astonished, and his mother said to him, "Son, why have you done this to us? Your father and I have been looking for you with great anxiety."*

*And he said to them, "Why were you looking for me? Did you not know that I must be in my Father's house?" But they did not understand what he said to them.*

*He went down with them and came to Nazareth, and was obedient to them; and his mother kept all these things in her heart. And Jesus advanced [in] wisdom and age and favor before God and man.*

Our Father, who art in Heaven, hallowed be thy name.
Thy kingdom come.
Thy will be done on Earth as it is in Heaven.
Give us this day our daily bread,
And forgive us our trespasses as we forgive those who trespass against us.
And lead us not into temptation, but deliver us from evil.
Amen

*For all lost and missing children:*
Hail Mary, full of grace.
The Lord is with thee.
Blessed art thou among women,

And blessed is the fruit of thy womb,
Jesus.
Holy Mary, Mother of God,
Pray for us sinners,
Now and at the hour of death.
Amen

*For grieving parents and families:*
Hail Mary, full of grace.
The Lord is with thee.
Blessed art thou among women,
And blessed is the fruit of thy womb,
Jesus.
Holy Mary, Mother of God,
Pray for us sinners,
Now and at the hour of death.
Amen

*For families who are estranged from their loved ones:*
Hail Mary, full of grace.
The Lord is with thee.
Blessed art thou among women,
And blessed is the fruit of thy womb,
Jesus.
Holy Mary, Mother of God,

Pray for us sinners,
Now and at the hour of death.
Amen

*For those who are separated from family for any reason:*
Hail Mary, full of grace.
The Lord is with thee.
Blessed art thou among women,
And blessed is the fruit of thy womb,
Jesus.
Holy Mary, Mother of God,
Pray for us sinners,
Now and at the hour of death.
Amen

*For those who are lost spiritually:*
Hail Mary, full of grace.
The Lord is with thee.
Blessed art thou among women,
And blessed is the fruit of thy womb,
Jesus.
Holy Mary, Mother of God,
Pray for us sinners,
Now and at the hour of death.
Amen

*For all who do not seek answers in the House of God:*
Hail Mary, full of grace.
The Lord is with thee.
Blessed art thou among women,
And blessed is the fruit of thy womb,
Jesus.
Holy Mary, Mother of God,
Pray for us sinners,
Now and at the hour of death.
Amen

*For those who do not understand God's words or messages:*
Hail Mary, full of grace.
The Lord is with thee.
Blessed art thou among women,
And blessed is the fruit of thy womb,
Jesus.
Holy Mary, Mother of God,
Pray for us sinners,
Now and at the hour of death.
Amen

*For all parents everywhere:*
Hail Mary, full of grace.

The Lord is with thee.
Blessed art thou among women,
And blessed is the fruit of thy womb,
Jesus.
Holy Mary, Mother of God,
Pray for us sinners,
Now and at the hour of death.
Amen

*That mothers will ponder the words of God in their hearts:*
Hail Mary, full of grace.
The Lord is with thee.
Blessed art thou among women,
And blessed is the fruit of thy womb,
Jesus.
Holy Mary, Mother of God,
Pray for us sinners,
Now and at the hour of death.
Amen

*That all children will advance in wisdom and age and find favor before God:*
Hail Mary, full of grace.
The Lord is with thee.
Blessed art thou among women,
And blessed is the fruit of thy womb,

Jesus.
Holy Mary, Mother of God,
Pray for us sinners,
Now and at the hour of death.
Amen

Glory be to the Father,
And the Son,
And the Holy Spirit,
As now and ever shall be,
World without end.
Amen

O my Jesus, forgive us our sins, save us from the fires of hell; lead all souls to Heaven, especially those who have most need of your mercy.

# *T*he End of the Rosary

Hail, Holy Queen, Mother of Mercy,
our life, our sweetness and our hope.
To thee do we cry,
poor banished children of Eve.
To thee do we send up our sighs,
mourning and weeping in this valley of
tears.
Turn then, most gracious advocate,
thine eyes of mercy toward us,
and after this our exile
show unto us the blessed fruit of thy
womb, Jesus.
O clement, O loving,
O sweet Virgin Mary.

Pray for us, O holy Mother of God.
That we may be made worthy of the
promises of Christ

O God, whose Only Begotten Son, by
his life, Death, and Resurrection, has
purchased for us the rewards of eternal
life, grant, we beseech thee, that while
meditating on these mysteries of the

most holy Rosary of the Blessed Virgin Mary, we may imitate what they contain and obtain what they promise, through the same Christ our Lord. Amen.

# *T*he Memorare

Remember, O most gracious Virgin Mary, that never was it known that anyone who fled to thy protection, implored thy help, or sought thy intercession, was left unaided.

Inspired by this confidence I fly unto thee, O Virgin of virgins, my Mother.

To thee do I come, before thee I stand, sinful and sorrowful.

O Mother of the Word Incarnate, despise not my petitions, but in thy mercy hear and answer me.

Amen.


In the Name of the Father, and of the Son, and of the Holy Spirit.

Amen

# $\mathcal{P}$rayers and Petitions

---

---

---

---

---

---

---

---

---